THE WOUND
of HUMANITY

Pastor Omojevwe Brown Emmanuel

Order this book online at www.trafford.com
or email orders@trafford.com

Most Trafford titles are also available at major online book retailers.

Printed in the United States of America.

ISBN: 978-1-4907-3332-6 (sc)
ISBN: 978-1-4907-3333-3 (e)

Trafford rev. 04/07/2014

Trafford
PUBLISHING®   www.trafford.com
North America & international
toll-free: 1 888 232 4444 (USA & Canada)
fax: 812 355 4082

To my LORD Jesus Christ.
And to Senator Boluwaji Kunlere, for his huge help toward
the needy. He is a role model—the epitome of humility.

Contents

FAITH.. 1

PREGNANT WOMEN.. 2

MONSTER OF HUMAN RACE.. 4

THE JOURNEY OF SOULS 6

THE ROOT OF EVILS.. 8

THE THIRD WORLD 10

MILLENNIUM SLAVERY 12

LEECHES IN POWER 14

NIGHT OF PRAISE..15

THE WORLD OF PRAISE..17

CRY OF THE EYES 19

THE SORROWFUL WOMAN 21

THE CRYING GROUND 23

DRIVEN TO FAMINE.. 24

DANCING HEADS 25

TEARS IN MY EYES 26

COLLAPSED WORLD.. 27

DRIVEN TO WAR 28

EMPTY NATIONS 29

ITCHING EARS 30

THE MORNING MESSAGE 31

BREAK THE WALL.. 32

THE GATE OF DEATH.. 33

PROTESTS FOREST 34

THE SNAKE 36

THE MADNESS SKULLS 37

THE LIFE OF NIGHT.. 38

EVIL SINGING MOUTH 39

HANG OUT... 40

MASKED FACES 41

THE FIRE...42

THE NOSE...43

I HATE LOVE..44

THE LIPS 45

THE HEAT 46

SMILING MONSTER 47

FORGOTTEN VOICE...49

THE WORLD OF FEW..50

THE SAND 51

VOICE OF CORRUPTION..52

I HATE THE WORD HATE..54

Acknowledgments

My special thanks go to the Almighty God for his unfailing love over my life and for His mercies and grace upon me, especially in days of trials, scandals, persecutions, and injustices.

I thank my lovely parents, sisters and my wife for their huge support, love, and care. I must not forget to acknowledge my lovely and beautiful daughter, Divine Okeoghene Omojevwe, for her smiles on my face daily, especially for spending quality time with me at night when I was writing this poetry book.

I acknowledge all those that contributed to the success of this work, people like May Brown (publishing consultant, USA), whose fingers are a colossus that makes publishing this book possible. Not only is May Brown my consultant but she is a voice that speaks out my name to the world of authors.

My special thanks go to the editorial team, staff, and management of Trafford Publishing, USA, for their corrections and criticisms that made the final work readable.

My special thanks to Chief (Hon.) Tola Wewe, Mrs. Elizabeth Boluwaji Kunlere, Hon. Moses Idiowa, Barrister Emeluaha Oghenekaro Stanley, the members of True Vine Evangelical Bible Ministry worldwide, and fellow co-workers in the vineyard.

I appreciate those who made financial contributions and those who pray for the success of this poetry book.

I also acknowledge all members of the poetry soup worldwide for their regular stop-by to visit my poems. Their comments have been so wonderful.

Finally, I appreciate the institutions, colleges, and individuals that would find my poems useful.

Introduction

Life is full of uncertainties; only those who have faith in God count it all joy. Having been through series of trials in life, I discovered that there is no person living on planet Earth without a dose of trials. Homes are made homeless, streets and cities are void of souls, earthquake has become a daily experience, and people are afraid of themselves. We all are living in a world where injustices and sufferings are broadly legalized, and credits are given to perpetrators of injustices while the suffering souls have no reward.

The poems in this book remind us of the need to return to our minds and trace every step missed because of stupidity, uncontrolled emotions, and greed, which led us to accept sinful offers from this world. Every child of God, irrespective of religion or background, had once experienced sad moments. These sad moments are the reasons for our daily cries and sleepless nights.

Humanity is constantly struggling with life, trying to find solutions to problems that our lust and greed created. Everyone wants to cross from the worse side of life to the influential side, thereby respecting sins.

In our circle of thoughts, looking at issues of humanity from a helicopter view, injustices and deceits are everywhere: in churches, mosques, offices, and colleges. The manslaughter of souls by humanity has turned the world into an unsafe place to live in. The voices of those who sing protection and security for citizens have turned to monsters' voices that kill, brutalize, and let down endless hunger and joblessness. Honors and recognitions are given to unmerited leaders of peace—the peace they hijacked and incarcerated.

The healing cream for this generation is therefore absolute or total turning away of our eyes from greed and lusts that this sinful world offers. Life will become more comfortable, peaceful, and lovely to live.

There is a need for everyone to consider as crucial human investment toward a better life. The time of sitting on the fence has passed. Now, we must disembark from the journey of making the hands of the poor suffer in the midst of the abundance around them.

Therefore, the need to read this poetry book stands as the only choice of advancement in positive directions that would give birth to a peaceful and harmonious society. It will drive home the rebranding if considered as an education material by colleges, public libraries, and private homes.

It will redefine minds of the unborn generations to follow the paths of uprightness. Finally, everyone owes his or her generation something worthy of praise; your right decision today will make somebody smile tomorrow. As your soul is important, so is the soul of another. Therefore, take all souls as important; your reward is either in heaven or earth, which will depend on the number of souls you saved.

This poetry book talks about reality, emotion, passion, helplessness, unhealed wounds of humanity, suffering, sorrowful mothers, and watery promises of leaders.

Also, it talks about the total neglect of humanity; tears that the rich and influential class never considered important. But their interest remained uncompromised.

In every generation, there are pharaohs that enslaved man, nations, or towns, and the spirit of darkness that manipulates or denied the poor their right to good living. Happily, the pharaoh of these people always goes down to their graves in the presence of those they enslaved.

The unmerited honor awarded to the influential and privileged individuals as well as their lifestyle are presenting questions in the minds of the suffering masses—but they are far from receiving answers.

Leaders' attitude of protecting their unjust rules, and blowing the whistle on bilateral relationship furthers greed and calculated starvation of the poor, instead of addressing their problems. They are busy receiving awards, recognitions, and honors than curing the pains they created on the planet.

The poems are not really my total life experiences or what happened to me, but those whose lives were unfairly treated in the society and sin's offer to encourage greed in humanity.

Eyes of justice are permanently closed toward sorrowful souls; leadership ears and few privileged followers refuse vibration of peace and co-existence.

The developed nations cross the Mediterranean Sea daily toward the developing nations in search of silver and gold in these poor continents for the developed nations to recover from their epileptic economy. The encouragement and support often received by these sorrowful women from the democratic dictators, their clever voice against communal conflicts, are to cement their interest in the Third World countries.

The reservation of oil-rich developing nations from clashes is to serve as "economic backup" to democratic dictators.

The poems also talk about hope for the hopeless souls, direction for souls, uprightness, fairness, justice, peaceful co-existence and living in fear of God. It is an eye-opener to those who embraced everything this sinful world offers without considering future consequences.

The symbiotic relationship between power and wealth of the super-rich—that send poor nations into slavery, hardship, and sanctions—needs to be broken.

The position of individual Faith in God will deliver souls from rolling in numbers into early grave.

The wealth of the few has become a bait that lets down millions into shallow, sandy graves, into deserts and streets of towns and cities. Finally, we all need to put our greedy appetite, hatred, wars, and sentiments to an end in order to eradicate confusions and killings across nations. Therefore, our collective campaign for uprightness and right living and submission to God's rules remain the solution.

FAITH

L ooking at the eyes of faith;
Its beauties run through my future,
I am reminded of my weakness in my ignorant world.
Looking unto Him; I saw nothing but my future's hand in His faith,
I came like those that lived by faith;
In beauty of faith, I was formed;
My Beauty is only but a resonance of His voice that speaks Faith.

Looking at the minds and eyes of every object of creation;
I see missing beauty that brought me to this world,
What is the joy of existence without faith in Him?
Looking at His eyes, my eyes get glued to its beauties;
Oh! Thou that showed me the path of life—look.
Look into my eyes and behold Your Beauties in me.
Yes, Your indescribable Beauty; running as the waters,
You came into my days.

PREGNANT WOMEN

As the sky carried the sun, the moon, the stars, the rain and the snow,
So you carried me in your womb.
In pain, in sorrow, sometimes, you carried me about.
You lost your girlish and womanish figures; just for me.
As the sky rains water and snow, so your body rains blood,
Just for me.
I delivered you into pains sometimes, which makes you uncomfortable.
But you never stop smiling in pain.
The fluid of your womb wall, never stop comforting me.
When I remembered your gentle touches and romances,
Each time your hands are placed on the ball shape;
I feel warm and happier the more.
The flood of tears in your eyes, the shout of agony;
Are furnaces of fire you went through; just for me.
As both legs opened, the eyes cried red;
Big sweat as pimples stood on her face.
I cried for my mother when I saw her in travail.
Who can be like my mother?

Mother! You died and resurrected during pushing; just for me.
You gave up your own life for me.
When I see how badly pregnant women are treated,
I remembered how she slept on her own blood and died.
Life, you are unfair.
Who can die to bring soul to life? Except my mother.
I shall put an end to the killer of beautiful mothers—pregnancy death,
You are a killer of happiness and joy in homes.
Many mothers are afraid of losing their lives, men are saying no to
baby-making; the world is crying for lacking babes.
I will not give sleep to my eyes;
Until mothers are released from pregnancy death sentence.

The house of life, that is what you are, mother.
Oh God, reverse the curse you placed on mothers,
How can she bear children in pain?
Have you considered her monthly discharge pains?
I cannot see them crying again in their labor room helplessly;
Oh God, if you refuse to heal women's pain,
I will refuse to bear female children; and never give me any.
The sky never cries or feels pain when the sun or moon is born day
or night.
Neither the fish in the sea during hatching.
Mother, life is meaningless, if I neglect you.
Pregnancy death, you are wicked.
I will work for all mothers' safe delivery; as I lived.

MONSTER OF HUMAN RACE

I never thought of ending my mission, until humanity traces their vision. I am the old apple, the gel of pleasure, sex is my name.

In my bitter, fast-ending world, you throw your hands of friendship around me.

I see the ignorant and indecisive look of humanity, as a fertile soil to bury talents.

The great and the small enjoy rhythms whenever they want to hurt me

You hurt me, when you cannot control yourselves.

I am furious, seeing you suck pleasures out of me.

I expose those that never stop sucking me dry.

You called me virus, but, honestly you made me look like your second skin.

Humanity calls me sin, when their friendship tastes bitter.

Who can say I hurt him or her? Humanity never stops hurting me.

Mocking eyes with tears, prayers, and curses, of the innocent,

Remind me of the unfortunate ones that you infected.

I never cause anyone pain, but humanity does.

As excited as life, songs, promises, and flowers are symbols.

You came into my life to hurt me.

Nobody knows when you secretly launched into my world.

I never sought anyone but humanity.

Why do you make me a casualty of your enjoyments?

It's your continuous patronage that paints sin on my golden name "Satan."

None sympathizes with me, even you that eat my fruits.
As degrading and pitiful my hard earned name, "Angel of Light"
I summon the courage to end the human race, for I know I have
but a little time.
Although am reminded of your zeal and ambition to dominate the
universe,
I am celebrated in the mind of those that wouldn't let me be.
Looking at the mind of humanity, I can jubilate.

Oh! What a world! The wise in the midst of blind minds and
blurred eyes.
Everyone has tasted me, few hate me.
If you can pluck out your eyes, without seeing my charming beauty,
I will not be hurt; you will not be hurt.
Looking into the future, I see humanity's irresistible lust and
demand of me.
Who can tell me the end of humanity chasing after my shadows?
The day you stop hurting me, peace will return.
But who needs peace more than I in this world?
Let humanity stay off me, there will be more dead in the streets,
than civil war massacres.
Oh! Thou that kill both great and small, great is thy power.
But greater is He that paid for us.

THE JOURNEY OF SOULS

I came to complete the works of creation.
In enthusiasm, all souls embark upon the journey of life;
Nobody knows the end, even those in the grave never return;
And tell the living grave's fairness and justices.
Under the scorching sun and thundering wave of conflagration,
souls restlessly labored.
Nourishments, protection, shelter, that souls labored for were once given;
But souls war against their lusts, journey of survival keeps increasing.
The seas daily lose their sands, the waters lose their volumes, the
earth loses its inhabitants, and souls lose hope.
Fingers and toes of souls are deeply on the sands; looks like scavengers.
Thoughts of all kind never allow soul to complete the journey
created for,
Some end up in hell, in prison of this conflagration world, while
some are still looking for where to go.
What planet will souls find humus to establish and end the journey
of pains?

The journey of souls is a tale of experiences: exciting and unpleasant.
I look disgruntled, disgusted, and disheveled in my appearance,
Then, I saw millions of souls disgorged out of the journey's van
into streets,

Crying for rescue; attention, and help that were never given.
As wide as the sea, its wave rejoices; as wide as soul's mind, its
thoughts rejoice daily on wickedness.
Souls' existence, does not know the length of her journey on earth.
Who can tell the dead the size of the grave where she sleeps?
Graved souls heard nothing but coolness hand of judgment.
Which is longer: the judgment day, the grave horror, or the
decaying bodies?
The dead knows not which is longer but wait endlessly.
If the soul begs to know the journey; the journey begs to know the soul;
Both are waiting endlessly, hoping to anchor one day.

How glad will souls be when pain and weeping shall be no more?
Singing, jubilations, and praises will house soul's mind;
When the merciful shall come.
Who loves the journey I find myself, me or you?
Or who will end my futility journeys:
My eyes glued to the cloud sky of heavens;
For hope is closer than ever.

THE ROOT OF EVILS

The source of good life is in me.
Man renamed me evil through their love for me.
You can call me money or woman; men love me more than I do.
I was crowned by greedy souls that never wanted peace in this world.
Everyone lost their crown for me, I rule the universe.
As numerous as my victims, none dare me;
Love of money is the root of all evils. Yes! They called I ; yet I am their hope.
Love of men and women for each other, give birth to my new name—root of all evils.
Look around yourselves, your possessions and respect for lusts kill humanity.
I am called money; with me you can fly, dance, sing, acquire possessions; and die in pleasure shamefully.
Oh! The greedy nature of men, is the root of all evils not me.
Men make me the root of all evils, when their desires to perpetuate wickedness wax great.
You tag me evil because you are irresistible to my commands

My love in your hearts, is the root of all evils.
Why do you love me more than yourselves?
None can restrain my love in their hearts. If the rich mishandle me,
They steal and kill the poor to have me and possess the world.
When they cannot work hard to have me, they cause wars to have me.
Those that never cared to love me, never hurt a fly.
I am in bondage and prisons where I am kept, feeling lonely and cold.
They stole me into secret private banks;
Waiting to be confiscated in the hands that never own me.
I am far from satisfactory love that I receive from humanity.

Release me, all hands have access to me.
Lust desires about me will die, when you love my creator.
I am abandoned in foreign banks where you kept me.
Making those that were supposed to add value to me lived abject poverty.

You place a band upon me; unjustified.
Those that wanted me in their hands in peace, never get me.
I saw ignorant ones dying in the Mediterranean Sea.
Oh! The influential, begs for civilized slavery—asylum.
The rights of the poor freeze in the deep freezer of the courts.
Justice loses its credibility, crimes increase, the law has imprisoned
the voiceless.
Judges seek for rewards, they placed the laws on the rich table and
reframed. Those who love me cannot resist my sinful beauty;
I am created to give equal life, but few deprived millions of
better life,
Out of the work of creature I was formed, but humanity made me sad.
Whenever they produce me with the blood of the innocent.

I am crying for freedom; Yes, freedom.
I was used as trade by barter thousand years, I lost my values,
The greed forced me into paper, and my value depreciated the more.
For you to carry me about; you forced me into plastic—
credit cards
What have I done to you?
I promised myself never to come back in the next world; if there
will be my need again.
Crimes I committed not; rather I settled. When will you pay for
your own crimes without dragging me to pay?
Stay away from me; you that love me.
If I fly away; the voices of the voiceless—the poor—will drop death.
The rich will have more slaves, more shall weep the urgent return
of the creator.
Austerity bailout will flow as flood on every land, blood of the
poor, the ground drinks.
Tell the rich to grant me freedom from wherever I am kept.
Yes, Freedom! I paid for everyone's freedom but nobody thinks
of mine.
Until the poor start to fight for my freedom, I will remain unhappy.
I am happier when the poor spends me,
In the private pockets, banks; savings for homes, there I am found.
The rich are the cause of my scarcity; spill their blood and find me
available again.
The rich are the root cause of all evil and not me.

THE THIRD WORLD

The crying voices, the tearful eyes of the poor, alive but not living.
A world formed equally but divided by crazy minds of wealthy and selfish.
If you formed first world, second world, third world, which class or world is God?
I woke up in my mother's womb, prepared by God for me.
I cried and smiled to every creature I met. Unknown to me, I am in a divided world, where the inhabitants are besieged by the rich world.
Confusion everywhere, endless bloodshed, terrorists attacks and sanctions, let down famine everywhere.
Who among the inhabitants of the earth can form first blood, second blood, and third blood citizens?
Even the knowledge of man has become destructive, distracted, and detrimental to himself and the environment.
Souls of the Third World go to their early graves.
Yes! Graves of the unjust, graves of sanctions, the graves of wars, the graves of infant bones of beloved ones, and the graves of the poor.
Everyone has seen the evil hands of the rich world upon the poor continents.
Oh God, why this silence toward men of "Distinct Color"?
Echoes of wars, fearful and helpless minds, loses power to selfish voices.
When the First World are driven by greed to acquire the wealth of the Third World.
Where is the love I saw when creatures welcomed me into their midst?
Sure, now I know that it was never love but pretense.
I am created as you are, both the Third and First worlds. God created them all.
Though, I may not be rich in my skin, but my mineral endowments are the pride of my color.
As dark as my skin, my wealth lies between my skin's layers.
No wonder, when you wanted me in your world, your distinctive color loses its pride and culture to me.
I saw the souls of the world whose wealth you stole, groaning in pains.
Crying because of hardship and starvation.
The land is continually wet with innocent blood, which no one thought of.

Poor but oil rich world, is now poor in oil but rich in poverty and
bloodshed.
I may not be significant as you though, yet I stand unique.
Who can tell which world will rule the world when the Messiah comes?

The continent is black, their skin dark.
Yet, their rich soil draws me into bilateral relationship; which they
do not represent.
My land no longer flow with milk and honey, but in endless wars
and sanctions
I pretend to be good, just to dig out their gold.
Yes! Of the Third World, irrespective of methodologies to silence
their voices.
As bad as the look of their skin, our streets full of flies that irritate
our eyes but grow our economy.
If I can't end the black race, I will continuously weaken their power
through sanctions and wars, until I dominate her.
What a world of Neocolonialism!
I am furious seeing the Third World crowed as raw minerals' king.
I may lose my control, if war seizes to spread over the oil worlds.

Though wars could take lives from my land, yet I will control the
First World.
Oh! First World, we are all casualties of your greed.
Famine, austerity, scarcity, and influx of immigrants in your world;
Are rewards of your greed upon your lands.
No amount of intimidations, wars, sanctions, frozen of bank
accounts which you supported to drain my continent,
Will force me to sell my people for slavery.
I see the Third World smiling in an ecstatic mood.
Your golden cities through your promises of help.
Help? Yes, which you don't and never wished to offer.
Listen, you need my help to recover from your epileptic economy.
In my vision, I saw the first class world get on their knees before
the lonely voices of dark skins,
Seeking for minerals to improve their economy.
I will remain a thorn in your flesh until you give me freedom.
Third World you call me, yet, I will remain the only leg.
You need to stand on economic stability.

MILLENNIUM SLAVERY

I woke up to find myself into a slavery of the day.
Bad memories of my fatherland lure me away.
Our leaders feed themselves fat, give empty promises, as the
years roll by.
Like a patriot, I fought to convince myself to stay, but had to go anyway.
Or was it my greed or quest for greener pasture?
Yes, I remember the sweet conversations of "good news" from
friends; thousands of miles away.
The beautiful pictures, hard currencies sent to me from the "better
world."
I fought to convince myself to stay, but had to go anyway.
But unknown to me, I was establishing what had been abolished
decades ago—slavery.

At dawn, the long unending trek under the angry scorching sun.
The horrific scenes of skulls and skeletons.
Stinks from half buried corpses in shallow graves.
The thirst. The faint. The convulsion.
And the death and quick burial of the weak.
And the journey continues.
At dusk, the cold blinding desert breeze, that stiffs the body joints.
The attacks from wild beasts, serpents, scorpions and mosquitoes.
Oh! It's not a nightmare but a kiss with death.
I have lost all my strength. Am better quiet.
Future where are you? I questioned in my mind.
With eyes wide awake, I peeped into the sky to beckon an eagle for help,
But none came to pick me away back home.
I hissed, after all, I established what had been abolished—slavery.

I woke up and say to myself, my fatherland why art thou unfair?
The whispers of intimidations keep singing into my sub
conscious mind.
Day and night foreigners lived with uncontrollable tears.
My feet recall, my hands frozen, and I was buried in the snow.
I shouted at the sky; the Eagle bird refused me lift.
If I jump into the sea, I will die in the bell of the fish, and;
If I steal to return home, I will languish in the jail of taskmasters.
Where do I go from here?
I woke up certain night and sleep refuse me. Thoughts of conscious
and subconscious mind keep me awake;
Then, I saw those minds, those names, those brains; that our
fatherland hope on.
Wasting away in the land where only certain color is dominant.
The spit of my father on the ground has dried, which reminded me
of several warnings.

I lost my father's land's right for millennium slavery.
Conscience becomes scarce commodity,
Dignity, the pride of our dark skin, loses its bond.
Dogs in the strange land victimize me,
I become an outcast in a land God made me to have
dominion over.
All black race, outside their fathers land, is a millennium slave.
Strength of freedom attached to slavery paper.
Those that acquired it, never think of returning home
What an era of self-imposed slavery!
Generations of black race had put themselves.
Even our descendants, are treated as second class citizens!
Yet, I am the pride of the world, the cradle of civilization.
I will arise and return to my noble world,
Where freedom refuses not its own.

LEECHES IN POWER

As old as the sand on the earth
So am I in power.
All colors leech on power
The dark loves me more.
Either you want me or not I will never flow in your direction
Those that want me to flow; frozen in their graves.
I decide when to flow; no fellow dares me.
Longing in corridor of power is life fulfilled
Nation with natural minerals, there you find me. staying power is
an honor worth dying for

Only those that follow me enjoy my current and waves
Yes, I made them rich and proud.
The fools thought all rivers are equal but some rivers rule others
I am the sea, the seat of powers.
I may be slim in size when I roar, ship capsizes. Yes, lives are wasted.
Flowing round the world I am fulfilled
Who can challenge me? Those in power I select them.

I fed them with fishes; support them with strength
If I flow out my seat of power, my leeching hand still controls power.
Go and tell the poor in the streets that rivers are not equal;
In power we are not equal.
There is no nation without me
Those in me enslaved others, rein their land
Though, you may not like my ruling
Yet I rule you happily and comfortably.
The waves of poverty, crises, and war of minorities
Never flow me out of power seat.
You fear no man but think about salt you leech;
As mighty as the leech, dare not eat salt
Oh! what vanity life you who stayed on power lived?
Leeches are in all nations' seat of power.

NIGHT OF PRAISE

I am created to serve Him, I am created to praise Him;
My praises to Him are my offering of sacrifices and
appreciation for being alive.
I was like them that dreamed dreams; when I was asked to come to
praise night.
Little did I know that 'I am created to offer sacrifices for all He has
done for me.
Night of praise, night of joy, night of feast. How sweet thou are?
When the living souls gathered in the feast of songs, worships and
in dancing;
How great thou are, night of praise!
When I remember His promises and goodness upon my life, I will
offer Him praises for the rest of my life.
Night of praise; How sweet thou are?
Sweeter than the honeycomb; Who can tell the taste, only those in
the night of praise?

I am created to serve Him and to praise Him till I return,
The stones, the birds in the air, the fishes in the waters, and the
plants in the land; they praise God.
The whispering of the early morning birds; near my window, woke
me up from my bed,
Saying: arise, thou that is sleeping, offer sacrifices of praise to Him
that created the day.

The sounds of the fishes in my little pond; where I rest in the evenings, say to me rise up, it's time for praise night.
Praise night? I shouted!
Thanks to my friendly fishes in my little pond.
How great art thou that created these fishes in my pond?
The parrot in my little golden cage, reminds me of praise night; His irresistible voice, keeps praising God for being alive.

Oh! Today is praise night, I say to myself.
What a night of joining hands with the Holy Angels to praise Him that eats only praises of the Saints.
I will feed my God with the praises of my Heart.
The tears of praises will not dry; until my praises bring down His glory.
When I remember His beauties in my life, praises will not stop flowing from my belly.
Praise night; night of miracles, night of wonders, night of total freedom, night of Holy Ghost experience.
When thou cometh, pass me not with Thy turrets of miracles, that are synonymous with the rain of praises.
Who can trade the night of praise for gold or silver?
No amount of promises in this sinful world can stop me from praise night.
My joy is in praising Him.

THE WORLD OF PRAISE

In this sinful world, the inhabitants offer no praises to the
Fountain of life.
A world of brutality, world of nudity, world of the blind and
the rebellious;
There I found myself. Yes! Self-created world that I once read about
in my ignorant days.
I was separated from the world of the living souls, though I was a
living dead.
My truant acquaintances in the world; where disobedient spirit
never allows us to praise God but condemnation of the saints.

Walking in the midst of the sinful, and the fearless hearts; I hear
sounds of rebellion itching my ears.
Every moment of my life, I found my soul going down to the land
of sorrows, and pains; even the help of the inhabitants gives no
encouragement.
My eyes keep wanting more of the sinful pleasures of life that never
promise peace.
The offers of this sinful world harden my heart toward
praising God.
Evil imaginations, never stop coming.
I became hostile to the saints that preach repentance to me.

In my hunting for sin, I found a piece of paper on the ground;
Saying: **"Praise Him! Praise Him! Praise Him!"** all the living
souls on the earth.
Then, I asked myself, who is He that I should praise?
Who are the living souls on earth?
Then several thoughts came into my mind;
But the voice from the paper wouldn't let me be,
The voice said: Praise the **I AM THAT I AM.**
It looks like a dream but it's real. Where do I go from here?
A silent voice sounding like rhymes said to my heart; go into my
sanctuary and join my saints in the Night of praise.
Night of praise? I asked the voice.
The voice resounded it harder that I cannot resist its force.
Night of praise, here I come to offer my praise.
I AM your Creator, **I** created thee for this purpose that my fame
will be heard through thy voice.
Yes! I will praise Him if nobody does.
All the days of my life, will I praise Him for his wondrous works.
World of praise where I belong; come quickly, souls of the Saints
are waiting.

CRY OF THE EYES

C ry of the eye; there is no eye without a cry.
Some pretend to love the earth in the midst of many troubles and cry.

The world, the sinful life and everything that dwell therein, make us cry.

The world where people cry. I belong not. The sorrowful mind, the jobless mind, the infants' minds that lose their parents to war; cried more than I do.

Who can say, the sinful life have not made him or her to cry?

Who has not lost his beloved to death, who has not cried; or sorrow has not greeted?

None! Not even you who has all that sinful life offers;
I will not be silent anymore.

Every eye has seen the cry this sinful world we found ourselves done, but everybody pretends to love their cry.

The painful cry women went through to bring soul to life; reminded me of life in the garden of Eden, where there was no pain.

When sin crept into man, women have to pay the price each time a souls wants to come to life.

The world allows both the righteous and unrighteous to pass through pains, sorrow, and endless struggles.

My eyes have seen the cry of those in pain, those bereaved, which the lust of flesh offers; to increase our stay and constantly make God unhappy.

I cry deeply in my heart each time man and woman break each other's hearts. Yes!

The uncontrollable cry of victims of love in sincerity.

My ears are tired of hearing of wars, hearing of death, hearing of sanctions upon nations.

The pain Muslim and Christian nations inflict on themselves has caused God's love to decline.

I ask myself, why can't witch doctor and occultist rise up and take over the leadership of the world?

God forbid! The world was formed in righteousness.

As I take a walk into the streets, enjoying the scorching sun, tears of people along roadsides; holding plate in their hands, begging for food and money.
I move closer to look at the plate, I saw smiles radiating on their faces.
I saw the emptiness of the plates in their hands;
What a world of hopeless hope?
My eyes run in tears,
I cried openly, until my nerves dropped off me.
My hope. My trust. My confidence. My enthusiasm about God declined;
Seeing inequalities and unfairness.

My mind bleeds when truth is incarcerated by greed.
Everyone has cried, in pretense, they manage life to live.
Where are the good promises of God for us?
In my brooding mood toward unfairness heard in the cry of people, life becomes consistently an uneasy journey.
I traced the cry in everyone's mind to greedy appetites of the rich, the politicians, the leaders, and the kings.
The noise about austerity, cry for survival, struggles to make it,
Hope, where are you, tears of my eyes has become iced block.
What is existence without good life? I hate wasteful existence but love eternity. Souls never realize how sweet is eternity, where there will be no cry, no pain, no sorrow, and no hunger.
The cry in our eyes shall be no more when the Almighty in fairness will judge the quick and the dead.

THE SORROWFUL WOMAN

Happily was I in your rib.
When I was invited to unleash man from his strictly
controlled emotion and loneliness of life.
My life with the man was more pleasant and adorable reaching the
climax of apogee,
Then man loses control over me and the lesser creature lured me
into sorrow.
Each time man loses control over me, I fall into sin with another man.
Woman of sorrow, is my outlook representation; inwardly I have
the cure for men's sorrow.

Impulses ascend and descend; sweats on my face tasted salty.
Tears from my eyes look the same as water in the bowl; but taste
differently.
In my awakening from the new knowledge saga, looking hastened
and excited,
I offered the excitement to the man.
What a good meal! The exclamation from his voice makes both of
us take a good look at each other;
What have we done? The creature replied: sin of course!
Words to defend myself became scarce,
The man in an aplomb mood, thinking of what to say, his mouth
closed,
His eyes read fear.
Then, His feet's sound vibrated in our hearts;
To imagine, how apoplectic and apoplexy His mind;
Is like one imagining the horrors of hell.
Then, I knew man has lost authority.
Sorrow greeted my face when His voice asked us to leave.

Life is unfair whenever I take a walk into my past,
How badly I was treated, molested, and raped by irresponsible men.
In my pains I still brought souls to life, yet sorrow has not stop
hurting me.
In my very eyes, souls I carried in my womb; are murdered in wars.
Each time I thought of settling down and helping the man to
achieve his goals, he breaks my heart.
Walking and complaining has not driven out sorrow from me,
But it opened doors for more sorrows.
I cannot seek for justices, if I do, the rich will buy the law.
Which one is better? My life without a man or man without me?
If I stay out of man's life, who will help him satisfy his pleasure?
Can life really be nice in absence of my existence?

To make up for the sorrow I caused man, I agreed to carry his flesh
and blood.
Yet, man never stopped treating me as trash.
What do I do to live without sorrow?
I'm an embodiment of happiness and love for man, yet man keeps
breaking my heart.
When he needs my lips, he kisses it and says goodbye!
The treasures of this world cannot be compared to me irrespective
of the way and manner you treated me.
I may wallow in the mud of sorrow, looking beyond the celestial
beauties of mine;
My fruit incapacitated men, if I refuse to offer it.

THE CRYING GROUND

I was never created to cry but created for joy; and to offer joy to them that tilled me for food.
Out of me came man; that is destroying me,
I am richly created but made poor and poorly treated.
How can you come out of me and still cause me pains?
Where will your dead bodies return and rest?
My riches, have I given to you; yet you are never satisfied.
In your greed, you milk me dried; cause me to cry.
Looking at the cracks on my beautiful face, it reminds me of your constant punches on me.

I have lost my happiness for you;
Bombs, oil spillage, chemicals, nuclear reactions, decays of the dead bodies you killed;
Have driven my wealth into extinction and the hope to be restored, far from focus.
Your sins have caused me endless tears.
When I see those that enrich themselves with my wealth;
Pleading to have a place in me to sleep, till judgment day.
I say, oh foolish man, thou has no place in me.
You can hang in between heavens and wait for your judgments for all I care.
Those who are yet to return, hear my voice and repent, I will deny some dead bodies;
The dead bodies of those who stole my wealth, happiness, and caused me pains,
If they sleep on me, I will deny them comfort;
They, who enjoyed much comforts in the world of greed.
I cry not for the rich whose bodies came to me with diseases; but those who were murdered in wars, hunger, and injustices.
In my cry to regain freedom, man is continuously destroying me;
In their pretenses, they embraced green eco to add beauty to me,
Stop your mass exploration,
Then, shall milk and honey flow out of me; and the cry for hunger shall be no more.

DRIVEN TO FAMINE

It is Incredible to see famine in the midst of abundances,
The cry for bailout package; is a designed modern robbery.
The animals. The ants. The birds; are demanding for bailout;
Protesting against hungers, neglects of man, and removal of famine.
What a world of protest and bail out we created for ourselves?
Sleeping with one eye closed and one leg opened; a new security
measure.
Land and sea that supposed to yield its kinds are famine.
We are all casualties, expect the air.
All creatures, fasting as a result of famine imposed on the planet.
Homes of the poor, hunger bites harder; ants find no crumbs.

I am driven to famine by you.
Famine made me to do what you all called terrorism, kidnapping,
suicide bomber that you once invented, supported, and protected;
Now condemned with one side of your lips.
In my famine, you employed me to destroy innocent lives and
properties;
You make more monies for yourselves when there is war
The more you drive me into famine, the more money you spend
and make;
Calling for famine; is like calling for war, calling for war is calling
for more dead.
Stop the war of the greedy; then, immigrants will stop floating into
lands.

DANCING HEADS

Heads are dancing thinking to share responsibilities.
The body can no longer carry the head.
Living heads are dancing about the roads,
Starvation has made the body unable to carry the head.
Heads become bigger than the body, as problems suddenly become bigger than the world.
The legs no longer dance but the heads do;
Some heads are dancing with epidemics that their nations caused.
While some are sup off in painful death;
Crying and shouting for help, the legs want to run from the body,
The heads run from the neck, bodies are headless.
Why do you sup off innocent heads; thou sword of the greed.
Tooth gnashing, as heads dance into shallow sandy graves.

Dancing heads of those who starved, looking dying; yet living.
Heads of those who are looking for jobs under the scorching sun, dances.
Heads of those in power seeking lasting solutions to hydra-headed menace that nations brought upon themselves.
Confusion everywhere as the heads of the learned, political guru, and mighty, can no longer sleep in comfort villas.
The head tells the body, hold me; else I fall off.
Heads are dancing into graves, who can tell whose turn will drum beat be?
A dancing head, if unhelped; is waiting—explosive.

TEARS IN MY EYES

Tears of the living and painful souls are in my eyes.
Tears of the children whose destiny has been robbed;
Tears of the youths whose right has been denied;
Tears of the old parents seeing their wards dying in the hands of
suicide bombers.
Tears of the animals on seeing their young ones dying of starvation.
My eyes are full of their tears.
If I don't cry their tears out, I may lose my sight.

Tears of the sea seeing fishes' bodies floating out of the deep to the land,
Tears in the eyes of the land, seeing dead bodies polluting her beauties.
Tears of the birds that are falling from the sky; begging humanity
to end shooting at the sky
Tears of the sand that is seeing millions of corpses in shallow little
graves.
Tears of the poor seeking for freedom that looks like mirage.
I can't stop my eyes from crying their tears, if I do, who will
understand that people have tears in their eyes unexpressed.

Tears of unborn generations that keep me awake all nights.
Tears of the innocent babes in the womb that will be denied of
their rights.
Tears of seeing images of God rushing to prayer for help;
Tears of nations that are suffering in the hands of monsters.

My eyes are dimmed, not because of my age; but because of the
suffering poor;
Ages have passed, attentions; yet given to their tears.
Each time I see tears in my eyes, I saw angry looks on God's face;
When will our tears be heard by God?
Looking down the streets,
I saw creatures' eyes pushing out from the windows;
In pitiful manner, begging their God for the return of Hope.

COLLAPSED WORLD

Things are fallen down, languages and cultures going into
extinction
Sky stood up with angry face, open her window and fall
Beauties of women have fallen great men
Collapsed their marriage and fames
Handsomeness of men has collapsed hearts of women
The wall of the world is collapsing daily
None to build it as it were before
Uncontrollable sexual pleasures of humanity grossly hammered
the world
Power from greedy souls collapsed the peace,
That was made as promise by God to man.
Oh! We are living in a collapsed world that her legs are amputated
By sex, poverty, greed, power, and unrighteousness; they hijack
the world
Collapse her and abandoned in weeping state.

Poverty led down wars, sexual trade and corruption were embraced
The abode of the poor is invaded daily by dangerous sickness
Collapsing the peaceful world we all cherish
Fear grips the young unmarried, sickness gradually forfeiting God's
plan for us, marriage.
Who can say he or she is not a victim of the broken world we lived?
Knowledge of man has collapsed the world
Where is the knowledge of God that framed the world?
Yes, we are living in a collapsed world
Lips of women have broken men's heart
Pocket of the rich men spray feelings around women's hearts
Homes are broken, religions are fallen apart
Nations are struggling to erect their feet
Who collapsed the world? All.

DRIVEN TO WAR

As the horse is driven to the streams so was I driven to war. Hardship in my mother's house drove me to war of hunting for survival.

In my father's tent where I was, you came and drove me to war.
The money offered; forced me to kill in the war that I never intended to fight.
Papers obtained with hardship that are wasting in my hands; drove me to war.
Driven to war is driven to sudden death; and driven to exile is driven to untold hardship.

My quest for justices and fairness in sharing of the national cake drove me to war.
I became like a woman approaching menopause; but yet to marry.
She is driven to war of hanging out with married men.
War everywhere! war everywhere!
Who cares what has driven me to war?
Hands of the greed have driven peace and love into an exile,
and war has suddenly taken her root down into the soil of human mind.

Everything in life has suddenly become a war, many are driven into spiritual war, physical war, and battles of unknown, just to make a difference in life.
No one is left out of war, we all are driven to war.
In my exile, I heard of various wars and murdering in my father's land,
War to obtain bright future in exile, seems difficult as the finger of war spread across nations.
Which kingdom war does not exist?
The kingdom of Jesus that shall come shortly.

EMPTY NATIONS

There is no river without lives; there is no land without creeping creatures;
There is no war without a permanent interest of the few;
There is no grave without a decaying body.
The sea will be empty one day of aquatic lives;
Sands are afraid of decaying bodies that sleep on it daily;
Rivers are rejecting decaying bodies; the rivers roared, float out of me thou innocent bodies float out of my me,
I throw up every moment I breathe in.
Nations are constantly destroying their brave men; women are running after the few left.
Little birds that patch on the branches of the tree are singing,
Don't empty your nation, live in harmony as we do.
Each time you sentenced, freedom is curtailed in your nations.
You open door for enemies;
Each time jobs are not created, new crimes are created, new graves are opened.
I saw an end of the games in powerful lands; when powerless lands love themselves.
Wake up thou sleeping lands, and stop emptying your human resources;
Those who instigated you, are raking your minerals into their land.
Return to God for wisdom and restore your land's wealth.
Say no to voices that gun down peace and love,
Then, shall your emptied land be restored.

ITCHING EARS

The birds are itching their ears;
  The monkey on bamboo tree, itching their ear;
  Waiting to hear peace in the forest.
When a man ear itches him, he looks around to pick up weapons for war.
Who can tell the meaning of the itching?
Sitting down in my raffia palm leave house, my left ear itches me.
Standing up from wooden chair, I rushed out to call my children inside.
What a world of fear all lived?
In a moment later, the itching sounds harder,
Leaving behind my children in the hunt, in a search for my wives.
Who can tell may be bombs from the sky; will drops in the bushes?

The itches continues for days, weeks, yet no sign of calamity
I couldn't resist it, I say to myself, it could be a sign of a good omen.
Inciting my finger into the ear, whitish substance followed my finger nail;
I shouted: Oh, it's milk!
Turning around to enter my hunt and lie my back on the wooden bed,
My little Dog that fear nothing but rain, laugh at me;
Fearful man that owns me for security, why are you afraid of itching ear of yours? Ran under my table, shakes her tail, yawned;
Humanity are not worthy living with.

THE MORNING MESSAGE

The poetic morning messages of hope, I grew up to meet; have gone forever from sight.
Gone! Now replaced with news of wars and killings;
Morning news has become uninteresting mostly to the poor.
Sunset that accomplishes morning messages with fragment smell of hope and excitements has gone too.
The sun, the moon look down into the earth; before setting, to avoid being bombed.
I grew up seeing my father's wives around him; listening to morning news.
This is the love I grew up with.
Waiting for exciting news of the day; the radio's poetic reciting was the culture that triggered my listening.
Morning messages are like oil that exalt my days,
The trees in the forest. The birds in the sky;
All listen to the morning messages and give praise to him.
Morning messages of praises, worships, and jokes;
I grew up with has been amputated by you.
What news do you hear today, we ask ourselves.
News of deaths and rape of women!
Everyone is scared to turn on their radio set;
For fear of being a victim of the news.

The voice of heroes and icons that wake up children from early morning bed;
Suddenly went into hiding.
Their voices gave souls morning messages of smiles and hope.
Creatures are crying restoration;
Children are crying; there is no more morning radio jokes.
Jokes and reciting of poems gone into extinction.
Morning messages that we all once relied on; how wonderful are thou.
Souls are awaiting your return.
I will come back from incarceration;
When you stop injustices,
Then, shall my voice play hope, and happiness again.

BREAK THE WALL

The wall of differences that tore us apart,
Keep standing in words of sightless and visionless minds.
As thick as the wall of our differences; resist the voice of colors.
Roofs are leaking;
The wall of greed that invented our differences;
When broken, new wall of patriotism, will spiral bound nations.
The walls of ancient values are falling and depreciating.
The wall between the rich and the poor gradually closing its gap,
As the roof leaked reports.
Break the walls, break the inequalities of colors on the walls,
All colors on the wall, spin story on eyes.
Break the wall of currency and build lasting wall of economy;
Break the wall of titles and retain honor.

Break the wall of rich and the poor; then the economy will spin
round quickly.
Erecting the wall of victimization; civilization stands no value.
Hands and voices are waiting to break the wall of ethnic divisions;
Wall of religious differences that spiral out tension and blood;
That make our salubrious world horror of horrors.
Who dares to break the wall?
Either they that erected it or those that will never forget the pain.
The hands of the incarcerated and those who bore scars of
marginalization are relentless.
The wall must be broken; either in peace or in blood.

THE GATE OF DEATH

I will shut my gate; and no man can open it.
And if I open it; all men shall come in once because of hunger in their world.
The bodies that entered me daily are unbearable.
The entrance of my gate has been battered.
Come with your money; ye affluence that desire my beautiful gate.
The weeping voices, bloodstain of the innocents and the curses that follow some death into my gates; Scared me.
I am only an entrance for your journey and not comforter of the bereaved.
I lift up my gates, for evil souls to enter without security check on them, yet they refused to enter.
They are waiting to snoop—on my gate; in my gate no detective enters and returns.
The imagination of hell kept many souls from dying,
The gate of death where only the dead in Christ dances for eternity.

My entrance is a sepulcher of peace for those who come in full age and lived rightly.
Gate of death where entrance is optional.
The faces of sepulchral, gloomy, and somber tones of voices of farewell never cease.
Footprints of the dead have broken my gate.
But the architectural splendor of my gate which split personalities; Whenever they come in contact,
I will shut my gate against unhappy faces; and corpses will walk freely with the living until the time appointed.

PROTESTS FOREST

Forest unsafe, forest unsafe, forest unsafe; wild animals outcry, evil spirits outcry, our kingdom has been invaded; let us stay with man.

Trees in the forests are having temperature; the anthills are bombed.
Animals are asking questions, where next do we live?
We have no hiding place again.
Rodents are running, insects are crying, scorpions and snakes are invading towns and cities.
Creeping creatures of the forest are encumbered with placards.
The wise toad and turtle choose to remain in exile,
Protests everywhere: in the forest, in the sea, in the air;
The dead are protesting for there's no land to bury them,
In the grave, the dead are renting bed space to sleep in;
As many bodies are buried in one grave.

Jumping trees with roots; hopping mad and feeling weepy; carrying placards.
Inhabitants of forests, time has come to pull down kingdoms, and time to build kingdoms;
Time for humanity to come to the forest has come, we are coming to town.

The centipedes and millipedes, and the rest of reptiles in the forest are crying from shortage of minerals.
The trees in cities have denied man comfort, though man planted us for comfort.
Stop your protests else we die! Man shouted as famines greet the world.
Small trees are breaking, as bigger trees march in protest,
Gods of the forest, why do you lose your potent power?
Relinquish your power and obtain honor.
Animals are dying, rodents are running, snakes are growing legs to run faster to the town.
Those taken as pets are warming up for war,
The toad cries out; my brownish skin is peeling, the fresh water is hot to stay.
As the trees that give coolness to the water are protesting.
The turtle went into its shell, thinking of changing habitation.
Voice of protesters singing horrible songs: Extinction! Extinctions!
Beautiful creature species are going into extinction.
Worms are waiting; waiting to devour all humanity that will die of hunger,
Forest, why help us to die? Death you said; stop polluting my world with missiles;
I, shall be fertile again.

THE SNAKE

I am the terror of the night; I am the terror of the day.
Fearful in the eyes of others, but friendly in fashion;
From my tail to the head, I am fearful and dangerous.
I am the longest creature on earth and sea.
In length, I am fearful to men; in bravery, man worships me;
I have neither hands nor legs, yet I move faster than man.
In the garden, where I was; man was my friend,
Until Satan borrowed my name;
In trust, I traded my name; future consequences flew.

I am neither the serpent that stole your dominion nor your enemy.
I am in pain as you are; why do you refuse to eat my meat?
Only those that know my values love my meat.
In your kitchen; I am unpopular.
I am the most valuable in your fashion world.
You don't remember that you once rejected me.
Oh God of creation, when will you hear my cry?
The world is against me. Who will vindicate me?
I need my name back: my honor, my legs, my hands, my friendship
with man;
I am created as you are.
If I have my hands and legs, man will not call me evil.

I am the pride of beauty, my products are world-class; speak volumes.
In the rock, in the forest, in the cities, in zoos, in your sitting
rooms, I am there.
If you feared me, stop buying my products, stop having me as a pet.
I have my own pains; as you do.
I never accuse man of not having legs or hands;
You accused me of your desires for lusts.
Oh my God, come with the wings of healing and heal my hands
and legs.
I am one of your creatures, look down upon me and wipe away my tears.
If my legs and hands are kept inside, how can I praise you as others do?
My shining skin, that added beauty to me are your works,
Looking ahead, my future's beauty reminds me of thy wondrous works.

THE MADNESS SKULLS

Standing skulls tear apart peace.
Necks that carry these skulls are longer in size.
Madness skulls look like gentlemen in disguise,
Learned skulls more madness than unlearned.
The birds in the sky have seen humanity's madness,
Destroy the sky; in your madness for power;
Where do you want us to stay?
If we build our nest in your beautiful homes,
You will complain of disrespecting.

Madness. Madness. Madness. We all are mad; but differently.
Some skulls carry liars and unrighteousness, some wealth and power;
Skulls that do miracles for mad skulls never heal their madness but appetites.
Other creatures like ants, birds, worship God;
Yet, no one hear their fighting, shouting.
The ants conduct elections, elect the queen;
Yet no blood shared in the election.
Fishes in the sea conduct election;
Yet the queen of the Coast has not lost her seat,
Nor blood of small fishes covers surface of the deep.
Other creatures are laughing at us,
Saying, what dominion do you have over us?
Madness in the streets, churches, mosques, and homes.
We have the skull you need to think.
Skulls of the learned erected walls of discriminations,
Skull of the unlearned occupied with madness of marginalization,
deprivation, sanctions, and equal sharing.
If the ants, birds, reptiles, worms, and wild lives lose their skulls;
Then the foundation of the earth will lose its gravity.
God save us from the madness of skulls.

THE LIFE OF NIGHT

L ife is in stages: morning, afternoon, and night.
Each stage comes with signs, codes of preparation; promises
and fulfillments.
Life is an embodiment of experiences; sad and good.
Trekking and thinking over old age life;
Life of night is fearful, and scary.
Life of night is like that of sucking babe,
Whose survival depends on the mother.

As fearful as old age life, souls commit to enjoy old age loneliness ;
Man walks on wide road of immoralities and injustices,
Buried their mind on fast lane life.
Looking at the brightness of the day; man playfully wastes his old-
age savings.
Life of the night depends on afternoon works and walks,
Life of morning looks greenish and promising.
Our walks and works withered the promises.
Life of night comes with cold and gnashing of teeth;
Only those that worked and walked uprightly; see old-age life friendly.

Life of night, my resting time, when thou comes;
Leave behind neither pain nor sorrow; for me to take into my grave.
Night is dark, life of night is dark; for those who played morning away.
Helping hands at night; distance in view,
When birds are signing and calling for return into their nest.
When doors of help are shut.
Everyone is afraid of old-age life that come in the night.
Life of night when bones are old; nerves collapse.
As fearful as you are, souls are refusing old age.

EVIL SINGING MOUTH

I am created for eating; to offer praises to God.
Many use me for trouble,
Some uses me for blessing and preaching the good news.
The wicked has taken singing from bird's mouth;
And from frog's mouth in the waters
I am given to you to sing praises and worship in his sanctuary.
Man openly sings out lies without looking for the reply of their lips;
Singing to gain favor, power, and recognitions,
I housed life and death.

Singing mouths roar to devour.
Some mouth rains coal of fire, curses, abuse.
Preserve me; and preserve your future;
To lose me is to lose your future and integrity.
Unbridled sings evil.

When my roof leaks, evil ones kill the innocent.
Listening to evil mouths is like digging one's grave.
I heal your presence; I heal your future.
I am your life; your life is me.
In a wicked voice; more news I spread
Only those that close to me, are wise.

HANG OUT

The tadpole hangs out with the floating cork;
Hoping to develop into desires, dreams.
In stages of life, humanity hangs out with sin.
Some hang out in bus stations, bars, night clubs, and under trees.
As flies hang on cattle's ear;
Souls hang their lives on wrong choices.

Hanging out at night is waiting for virus reports;
Hanging out with masked friends; is walking with death.
Uncountable souls are down like ship;
Influence of me has made many sorrowful.
Waving my hands to hangout life,
Cost me tears that I never intended;
Her watery promises; her beautiful, but destructive offers;
Remind me of my walk into her.

Souls of hangout life, standing as beheaded tree; that waits for rain
water to drink.
Yes, rain.
Who will rain the gospel into me?
In my world of wasteful, painful, sorrowful, and hopelessness.
The spirogyra hang out on waters' current, yet died.
The waters dried, and water birds devour them.
Who can tell the next victim of hangout life?
As waste as the head; so also the ears that follow it.
Life of hangout is as wasted as spits.

MASKED FACES

Faces are around you; you are around faces,
We all wear mask on our faces.
You mask around me; I mask around you,
Yet, our symbiotic living unmasked.
Masked faces are friendly in appearance but fearfully represented.
Remove the mask, the heart beats faster;
As harmless as nose on the face, so looks masked faces.
Whose face is free?
Lusts drove faces to mask.

God of creation why is your face not wearing a mask?
In all ages, I was.
Faces that pray daily; mask of lustful desires.
Masked faces stand as epiphytes on memory.
Masked faces are everywhere; like air.
Time to unmask masked faces,

Living with masked faces is like staying with the talkative.
Who can tell whose face is masked or not?
Only God knows.
We all are masked differently.

THE FIRE

I am power and authority; fearful in appearance.
No one makes me a friend, have but one enemy: water.
In my world there's no correction,
My actions look insane; yet no blame.
I am the power of love in men's heart;
If I quench, love dies and tears let down.
In my house, splendor of smokes increases my joy.
Both small and great worship me.
No one dares me and be alive, not even the iron that melts in my presence.

Everyone that loves me; carefully handles me,
Without me the wicked rules the righteous.
I rule in justice and fairness,
Entering my court you need to think; for my judgment is irreversible.
Woman that knows my role in love; seizes men's heart.
I am behind love emotion, watery promises hover on the lips.
I regret the day when water was created.
You can swim with your enemy; who dares swim in me without getting hurt?
Humanity fears me than the enemy.
Water, why thou came?

Oh! How glorious is my potent power; that will end all wickedness.
Judgment comes quicker; I am hungry to see skins worshiping me.
For this purpose I was created to destroy wicked souls.
Seeing Satan melting like wax, gives me honor;
Without me, the wicked will turn into fish, and swims out of judgment throne.
I am called consuming fire, that is my name.
Nothing can burn me. I burn all things; I cook all things.

THE NOSE

I may look ugly as two holes are in me.
As the mountain cannot be hidden so do I on the face.
Standing on the face; more beauties are added;
Unseen by eyes and mouth;
I am the path eyes take to the mouth.
If I refuse to act; the mouth will not eat;
If I decide to move out of faces, faces become uglier.
No matter how ugly I may look, no one dares cut me off,
I smell sins before they are committed.
As sensitive as I am, no sin passes me by.

Take me away from the face, sin will reduce.
Block the nose, speech of man will be unclear; there will be confusion.
Cut me off, sin shall be reduced.
The two small holes of mine, secure myself from harm.
The swine valued me, and lacks nothing.
I made myself dark on dog's faces; he became a perfect detective
than man.

I am tired of being used as a detective;
The eyes see for man but I deceive man to take . . .
Take what? What I smell.
Sitting on the face; displeases me.
I am delicate; and fragile never you exhaust
Some exhausted me, and ask for plastic surgery
I will refuse to sit on the face.

I HATE LOVE

Love, I hate you but you pretend not seeing me,
Those who love you are like you, killed by you
Through your firework many had paid with their lives.
The rich and religion leaders speak of you
Yet they kill and steal to have fun around.
Who really loves? The world or the inhabitants?
I will not love until genuine *love* comes.
In genuine love was I created and loved but imperfect love,
Created hunger, greed, evil desires, bombing, and terrorism.
I hate those who love in pretense.
Love of the lips has killed my thirst for love
Humanity loves yet they break each other's heart,
Women, drink you daily like water; speak of you more than God,
No home that does not weep of your evil deal.
Souls are waiting for perfect love that will care again and are
freely given
I will be at peace with love if colors love without harm.
I hate you since humanity will not stop using you to destroy.
Oh, love of God when will you return?
Souls are waiting for your voice of caring and equality,
When you come, I will love again.

THE LIPS

O h! what a world of sin I created?
    Looking around humanities, I saw the beautiful lust in
    their heart toward me.
All big teeth, considered me important.
I cover the teeth no matter how big it may be or the decay particles
that hangs on;
Women painted me to lure men into destruction and say good bye
to their senses.
With me in colors, men lose their heart for women;
Yes, once contacted me; contract is signed, feelings rains.
Without me, men will not have women's heart; or look at their ugly
but charmingly faces.
I make faces more beautiful; mostly when in colors. No face can
shine without me.
I am the spice of beauty; catch a glimpse of me, emotion, pleasure,
feelings will smile back at you.

I am the bridge of love, you can't destroy or ignore me; and still
climb into full atmosphere of lust and deceptive.
The women knows my important in schooling men around; plug-in
into each other; is likes poles, my attraction is confusion.
Throw a finger across me, disagreement will be silent; and contract
will be signed.
In my world of deceptive, decent life is a mirage.
I can make good, I can kill. Rushing your mouth into me; risk of
deceptive, pains and weeping is high.
I am the sepulcher of souls, no matter how you painted me with colors,
I change not but many souls lust after my colors.
I appeared good to sinful eyes that wouldn't let me be, wisdom of
knowing my nature is total abstain from using me to kiss. what do
we kiss with or eat with?
No matter how worse is your nature, Lips, stay on my face. and
make my morning and bed time like rose-garden where faces forget
their identity in God.
Until you stop painting me to achieve your evil desires, I will
remain the only tools of confusion in this world.
I will allow humanities to use me to break each other's heart.

THE HEAT

Heat to make it and perish is rising like sea waves.
Heat of politics is making many sweat like iron in the furnace;
Sweating profusely in their private jets;
To deliver perforated speeches of empty promises.
Everyone is heating up their blood to kiss riches;
The rich are heating the poor; men are heating the women hard;
And women are heating every corner of the town with love.
Men are heating women's heat with deceptive love;
Heat of lust has a generating power; gives illumination to souls.

Heat of the devil on humanity to take their dominion again;
Has sung songs of blood flow, starvation, unrest, and various epidemics.
Famous spirit is another heat in our leaders; spilling the blood of innocents across continents.
Heat up the family with unnecessary demands; men become mad, confused, and promiscuous.
Heat the nations; things will fall apart. Heat up power seat; heads will roll.
Heat the churches with prosperity, bigger congregation will emerge.
What a world of heat we all lived in?

Heat of hunger everywhere, heat of bail out, heat of returning to power; sending fear into the minds of the weak.
Heat of prosperity crusade in churches is a trademark of eloquent preachers.
Heat of crimes among the super-rich; has suddenly become a red carpet show,
Heat of signing gay gospel bill into law by nations; and say goodbye to cultures, values, and integrity;
Many looking at the sky for the return of their Creator.
The heat of hell, no longer scares evil and famous men;
Either in hell or on earth.
Waving my hands of goodbye to all form of heat of this world;
My peace returns.

SMILING MONSTER

The earth shakes; rivers are drying, air whispering tears;
Trees are afraid of standing outside, as warplanes
hovering.
The ground is running from bombing and shooting,
Houses begs for legs to run from bombs;
Dead bodies of humans has become like sands everywhere.
You kill them; you adopt their children; you advertised innocent
children on medias
Calling for money donations, children are crying; women are in sorrow.
Little children are crying; stop using us to beg for donations,
You made us homeless and parentless
What a world of monsters! Caused by greed.

Little children's cries on the streets and camps seized sleep out of
my eyes,
Going to my comfort bed has become sorrowful,
When I see millions without bed to sleep on, no food to eat
But feeding on flies has become daily diets.
You tear apart our lives; when we didn't prepared for it.
You are happy; using us to beg for donation and aid;
To show charity and love, which you can't offer.
Our swelling stomachs, faces, and legs are malnutrition inflicted
on us by you
Monsters! Monsters! Monsters! Is what you are.

Little children are crying, crying, crying . . . wanting their voice to
be heard.
You stand in front of your co-taskmasters and those alive but not living;
Promising comforts and cares; Which you offered in disguise.
When wars and killings you planned have not stop,
Missiles are dropping at our backyards.
Lies hovered on your lips each time you promise peace.
In fears, and uncertainty, we sleep on dried leaves openly as animals;
Yes! Animals. Your bombing smoked us out of our homes into camps
Where you capture us for second slavery.

Which death will I prefer?
Death of chemical weapons, or death of fearful bullets;
Or death of starvation, or death of homelessness or death of joblessness?
I am afraid of the death of slavery imposed on me.
Oh God come and fight for weaponless souls,
Send your arms of justices quickly, else your beautiful earth will
be void
Of your image.

FORGOTTEN VOICE

I am forgotten by others: the voice of the rich and the powerful.
Forgotten where you sent me
In faraway war, in the sorrow, in the wilderness of pains, in
the prison of injustices.
The juggles where I am begging for attention.
No bird listens to my voice,
The tree they build and perch on, was planted by me.
The lonely grave of dead voices grooming in sadness
I am forgotten out of minds.
None remembers the blood of freedom I fought.
I spilled my only blood for justices.
I shall cry until you hear from your rich world and wickedness.

The voices of raped and impregnated women,
Are abandoned to wallow in tears, oh, what a helplessness
The weaker dusts find themselves?
Denied of love and happiness, frozen between options
I have no more strength in me; to shout for hearing.
Who will help my voice and cry my cry for remembrance?
I have no son in the class of the rich to wheel my feelings.
In the world where poverty is an unforgotten epidemic,
Once infected, forgotten in the dark;
Like a condemned inmate, yet hope on fate someday.
The hands of corruption crucified voices of iconoclasts.
Silenced me in the grave of tears and helplessness
The land where I lived; only forgotten souls crossbreed.
Where fighting for equality and justices bed our minds.
I am kept between thoughts,
Thoughts that my voice will be heard on revolution
When the voice of all souls shall be heard on holy throne.
Thou that hear the voice of the afflicted and oppressed
Remember me early.

THE WORLD OF FEW

World of few friends. World of few homes. World of few clubs;
Where greed, power, and sinful appetites are the roof.
The few rule and cow around inhabitants in pain and sorrow.
I recognized no equality, no peace, no justice, and no freedom
My foundation is built on selfishness,
Greedy appetites of the few hijack the peace world.
The world where their guns rain poverty, kill little children on streets, under trees.
Multitudes are driven into captivity, and never return.
They shake nations; turned against the godly.
A world where public funds flow and float in the direction of the rich.
Ruled by the few, letting voiceless voice into graves
My plans, yes, my plans, peace shall be no more.
Looking down on the world of the few,
I saw Lucifer beautifully decorated in apparels.
Boastfully dressed, worshiped by those who possess worldly possessions.

The world where poor bloods are waiting endlessly for redemption.
Each time I look into your eyes, my fears, I see no more;
In your lusts, you increase the happiness of my adversary.
All voiceless and sorrowful hearts; prepare for my return.
The world of the few, will I uproot and plant another.
Bloodshed is a cymbal in the world of the few.
Corruptions and injustices are their dance,
Surely, all muted voices shall be glad at my thunder.
World of peace, love, and fairness run for restoration.

THE SAND

I may look ugly and formless; my importance unbeatable.
My memory is as smooth as the blood
No information elude me, all the dead in me are beautifully
ground into powder.
I am not merciful neither friendly, all that came from me I swallowed
Foots that run to shell blood; know not my wickedness.
Though, you stood on me, and you build on me with ungodly wealth,
No one thought of my surveillance's usefulness
I watch you wherever you go.
Sand, that is my name. You carry me about in your bodies;
In your car, in pockets of your wares, homes, offices, I am there.
I made you, I also eat you at will
No soul has control over my power,
I am a part of you, you are a part of me.

As ancient as history, respected me
I have reliable information about souls
Those who buried corpses secretly on me
Never thought about my uniqueness.
No history of evils or good elude me, not one.
If you what any information about souls, visit me
Those who visited me, never return; they become a part of me.
I am sand, I kept dead bodies when they died
I am a part of the living.
I never engage in evil acts, but help humanity to hide evil.
Let those who do evil, remember in due time;
Time to reveal openly all evil doers.
When all the dead shall come out of me.
I am as old as the world herself,
Before good and evil were created, I was.
Look at me, what do you see?
Holes where your decayed bodies will sleep.
Nothing is as valuable as me
I cover the dead with my shinning clothes, called sand.
Look under your feet, I am there.
I know your history, but mine, you do not.
Before the coming of my valueless
When souls shall live with angelic body.
I will remained your lord
I vowed never to relent to cannibalizing souls.
Sinful souls shall remain in me for eternity.

VOICE OF CORRUPTION

As the tree branches out its hands to collect wind
So do men branch out their hands to offer and collect me
willingly.
Sweetness and bitterness of life are my darkness' works
Those who eat from me are those singing the song—let's stop
corruption.
Who can say, I am the cause of drought in all nations?
Everywhere, echoes of your senseless possessions, crippled the lands
Look inside you, you will see corruption's seed happily growing.
Color of skins, no longer fears but trends on my path.
Some kill to magnify me; some are roped into my wide name.
The mouth of the corrupted wants me stop for better life
Better life they never intended for any living soul.

I am everywhere: in the church, in the mosques, in the families, in
the schools;
Even in the bedroom of individuals. I am there.
As the nose stood on the face, so do I; in your mind
What you do not need; you do have them.
You give birth to me daily in your blood and tongue
Your eyes see me and are glued to me.
To end me, is to end all humanities; all have corrupted.
Who can say I am not a part of him or her?
The only truth in your mouth is me.

I am the bedrock of distinct color's economy
I made them rich and kept others' borrowers.
I made some rich, I made some rotten in jail, while some are
permanently poor.
Famine, marginalization, mass death; strengthen my existence and
co-existence.
I walk through dispensations till date.

Those who enjoyed me pervert the course of justice and fairness
Oh, thou that eat from my table, why do thou want me sentenced?
Has thou considered: your husband, wife, children, and friends
who I fed fat?
I have come to stay in this world since man never thinks to stop
wanting more;
You called me corruption, but I called you my seed.
I am god to the rich and enemy to the poor.
If I smile to your faces or hands, no one can resist and flee
I gummed your eyes and palms as the fluid in the bone.
I am due for legalization and honor, then peace will be restored
Honor me as you do for those I made.
Having headaches daily on how to end me
Never stop me from living in the heart of greedy men.
I need recognition; sign me into law worldwide.

I HATE THE WORD HATE

As a rain you drop from the sky slowing into men's heart
Weaken our coexistence, creating factions
The way leaves of plants droop down; rotten, smelling
everywhere; so do you.
Rotten mind against minds; parading evils where you are found
The rain of bitterness, wars, killings, greed are your droplets that
beat the roof of our mind and soul
Hate, you draw hatred lines; dress the stage for evil to act

The word hate has whipped homes, torn apart mutual friends,
divided nations; spilled the bile of many.
As the insect crawls into honey; so you crawl into souls making
happiness lifeless.
In marriage, divorce gums unfaithful men's heart
The divorced carry hatred like the face that carried the nose
I say in my lonely cave, hate, what have you done?
Hate, you fall and grow on soul's mind like a seed;
Letting wickedness crystal round single thoughts of man.

In every man's heart you have a room to lie your head
Our daily endless war was let down by you.
War everywhere, death everywhere, hunger everywhere, hate
everywhere; you fathered all evils.
Some painted me on their lips; while others incubated me in their heart
I flow like endless river in your thoughts; as long as souls lived,
forever I rule thoughts. all colors, skins; practice me.
Those who hate God's uprightness and holiness, made laws that
rain more hate into minds, instigating wars in peaceful nations.
wives hate husbands, children hate parents
Citizen hates their leaders, even hate themselves.

I rule the mind of the wicked, no wickedness done without me
Flashes of me burns than fire, flooded than mighty river that breaks wall
If I roar, souls quivery; only love can cure me but who love who?
My continuous existence; increases sorrows, pains, wars . . .
Take me away from your mind, thoughts; then equality anchored.
In a busy world that hate uncured, greedy souls oppress
The kernel of hate hard to break.
Everyone trying to find cure to many things;
But no one is able to cure hatred from souls.
I hate hate; made me friendless
Why are you always in me when I don't want you?
Religious hate themselves, nowhere is safe to go
Powerful nations hate the lesser ones.
In pretense, communication appears friendly but hatred butts up.
When I thought about hate, I hate hate the more.
Those who create you in their world; never thought of future
consequences.
Hate, as I lived I will hate you.

About the Author

I was a great sinner, committing all kinds of atrocities. I never went to church; I was a womanizer and blasphemer of the gospel of Jesus Christ. Now, I found grace, repentance, forgiveness, and perfection. I am prepared by grace, honored, qualified, chosen, accepted, and cleansed by the blood of Jesus—I am now a preacher of the gospel that I once condemned.

Pastor Emmanuel Brown Omojevwe is a recognized and respected pastor, founder, and General Overseer of True Vine Evangelical Bible Ministry worldwide. He is based in Italy, where the headquarters of the church is found. He is a prophet, teacher, evangelist, pastor, preacher, prolific writer, poet, and an international public speaker. He is a man whom God is using all over Europe to anoint, deliver, and bring transformation in the lives of millions. He is a husband and father to millions, a humble man of God who believes that God can use anyone irrespective of his or her sins, circumstances, and backgrounds as long as he or she is pruned by God.

His desire is to preach the gospel of Christ to all nations so that peace could be obtained and the body of Christ is unified. Also he is of the opinion that materialism gospel should not be a focal point of a true man of God.